Anchor Light:
An Awakening of Your Greatest Treasure

ANCHOR LIGHT

An Awakening of Your Greatest Treasure

**From the Teachings of Paul Wyrostek,
Channeler of Healing**

**Written by
Diane Allison Beyersdorfer**

Art by Caleb Allison

Imagination with intent through love is the key
to manifesting the life of your dreams.

Mill City Press, Inc.
2301 Lucien Way #415
Maitland, FL 32751
407.339.4217
www.millcitypress.net

Printed in the United States of America

ISBN-13: 9781545617267

Table of Contents

Paul

Being forged through fire may seem harsh, but, like steel, it creates a force within that can't be broken.

In this lifetime, perhaps the biggest lesson I have learned, is that we are so much more than we think we are. We are more powerful, more beautiful, and more magnificent than our eyes allow us to see. What I want to tell you is that there really are superheroes in our midst. They walk along-side of us, and many times they were born in to a very harsh environment to prepare them to be the empaths, counselors, teachers and healers of our time. Paul is one of those people. Not only was he born into a home of neglect, abuse, hunger and fear, but he also was born a wide-open medium and empath.

We all love scary stories told around the campfire. We love the chills that run down our spines as we imagine a big scary monster sneaking up behind us in the dark. We may not get a lot of sleep that night, because those stories may turn in to our nightmares, but, the next day, when the sun comes up, the fear is replaced with a few good laughs and we go on with our lives. We are totally oblivious to the fact that the scary thing we imagined coming up behind us the night before, was actually real.

1

For a few select people on this planet, those scary stories play out in real life as they try to walk through a living nightmare. They can actually see the monsters that hide in the dark, and, because of that, the monsters often seek to destroy them. Paul's life story would rival movies such as "Poltergeist" and "The Amityville Horror". He not only did survive, but I believe that because he was able to overcome such huge darkness, he has now become a huge beacon of light for so many.

Many of us feel alone. We feel as if we were abandoned on an alien planet. Paul was no different. From the time he was very small, he remembers the horror of being left someplace that he didn't belong. As I listened to Paul's story, the most beautiful part was that, even when there was incredible pain and suffering, he was never alone. Through it all, there was always a light, a spirit guide, or a team of angels and Ascended Masters. They were always behind the scenes, sometimes just to light the way, and other times to pull him out of harm's way. In his own words, "I began to trust them because they became like fellow soldiers on the front line of battle." He has developed a strong bond with his spiritual team and through that bond, they created a way to channel healing that is uniquely effective.

It is through the extreme pain and darkness of his younger years that Paul's eyes are wide open to the difficulties that his clients experience. He not only is leading people to the healing they need, but also teaching them to create a more intimate relationship with their own spiritual teams and with their own higher selves.

It is no mistake that you are reading this book. If you are drawn to the words on these pages, you are being led to healing and to a place of greater understanding of who you truly are.

Diane

"Transformation occurs when we allow it and to the measure that we allow. It only requires love. It is in fully loving yourself that you are able to transform into everything you are capable of dreaming of, and more than you can ever imagine."

In many ways, my life is no different from so many others. I lived through a lonely childhood, an abusive marriage, and then the loss of my love to cancer. I am not so different from you, or I wasn't. The one thing that sets me apart is my need to grow, to expand, and to become everything that I can possibly be. I refuse to live in a low vibrational energy that pulls me down into the muck of everyday life. I choose to live a life that is full of joy, of purpose and laughter.

When my husband died after a very short fight with cancer, I thought my life was over. I wanted to curl up and die quietly to end the pain. He had other plans. He never left me, not for even one second. He set about picking up the pieces of my life and bringing people to me that would help me find my way out of the pain and darkness.

Paul Wyrostek was one of those people that Steve brought to me. After my first session with Paul, I began to change and with each session thereafter, I became more and more aware of who I truly am.

It didn't take long to realize that so many of us are walking down similar paths. We long to find others who feel like home and when we do, we find comfort and we begin to transform. I am not the person that I used to be, and I am so thankful for that. There are steps in life, and when we become aware of those steps, we realize that our lives are like puzzles. With each new step, another section of the puzzle falls gently into place.

There is such peace in this process and it is not difficult or painful at all. It is the process of letting go of the person you think that we are, in order to discover who you

really are. I am here to tell you that who you really are is so incredibly amazing that once you fully uncover yourself, you will wonder how you got through life for so long without truly knowing yourself.

Let this book be a treasure map for you as you gently set your ego aside and read each page as if you are that little child who believes in buried treasures, swashbuckling pirates, damsels in distress, dragons that fly, and adventure on the high seas.

Savor each page and know that by the time you reach the end of this adventure, you will have changed. You will be closer to becoming the magnificent creation that you truly are. You are so loved and I hope that you will feel the love that I have instilled within these pages. If you are reading this book, you now embarking on the journey of a lifetime. Let the adventure begin!

Caleb

Think about where you are in your life right now. Alright, you got it? Now, think about where you want to be. Anchor Light is the path. You won't come out the end the same as you were. You're going to face some harsh truths and you're going to remember those rough times. But, to make this book happen, an adventure occurred. I hopped on a plane for the first time; alone and anxious 37,000 feet in the air. My destination was Boston, where I'd be greeted by my aunt, Diane, and by the brains behind it all, Paul. I remember when I managed to find my way through that labyrinth of an airport, camera in hand to find them both. Diane hugged me and Paul shook my hand. But, Paul's first words to me weren't the typical, "Hey, I'm Paul." No, the first thing Paul said to me was, "How was your flight?" Like he was asking an old friend. Part of me thinks he might have been. The adventure took us up and down the Massachusetts coast. We saw incredible things: castles, beaches, and so many beautiful dogs. Anchor Light didn't exist yet, but as the week went on, we could feel it generating in our hearts, changing who we were. I was, for certain, a completely different person before I got on that plane. But, once I allowed the concept of the story to change me, it did. Monday the weather was a groggy, confused mess. By Wednesday, it was 70 degrees with a few clouds. But, by Friday, it was perfect. That was the last day we had before the squad split up to get our individual pieces put together. I came back a new person. You're reading the prologue now. You are me; a young, naive, lost human about to take a journey. Are you going to allow it to take control and change you? Or, are you going to hold onto those old pieces? For this book to work, you have to allow it. Feel it, believe in it. Take control. If you doubt yourself for a second, remember: you are made of star dust and Godly intentions. Believe in yourself and get back to reading. One more thing, Diane, Paul, and I are with you in every chapter. Just look out for us.

The Ship's Cook

I see the ship's cook. A pile of onions laying before him along with carrots, potatoes, and fresh fish. This stew will be fit for the captain. The ingredients were hand-chosen for this purpose.

As he reaches for his first onion he silently prepares himself for the tears that will surely come. Layer by layer he begins to peel away the skins. The first layer is frayed and it peels away easily with almost no resistance. The second layer requires a little more effort but soon it is gone to reveal a more beautiful layer underneath.

He patiently continues with a few gentle words to this special onion that he chose from the huge pile. While this onion may not have looked like much when he began, he knew from the feel of it, that underneath all of those layers, he would find perfection.

There is no rush in his work. A soup of this caliber takes time. Layer by delicate layer, his onion begins to reveal itself. The fragrance is divine. The color is perfect and at the very core is the heart of perfection.

Like the onions in this story, you too have been chosen by hand. With every layer that gets peeled away, you come closer to that perfect light that you came here to be.

It is not the process of changing you in to something brand-new at all. It is the process of helping you to return to who you were when you arrived into this lifetime. It is peeling back the layers until you finally dig down deep enough to remember the shining star that you truly are.

Captain's Log: The Ship's Cook

Each one of us comes to this planet ready to complete a mission even if it is just a life time to heal and rest from past lives. That can even include past lives from other planets or dimensions. Years of neglect, pain, abuse, or just survival, have built layers of damage that cover the pure golden white light of your true self.

Healing sessions usually begin with the most recent layers of pain or the blocking energy that is holding you back from your truth at that time. but with each consecutive session, there is another layer exposed until there comes a day, when that pure, beautiful heart of yours is revealed.

Each one of you is here to carry the light to the rest of the world. With each layer that is shed, your light begins to shine more and more brightly. You will find that, in time, holding that light becomes easier and easier for you.

It really is all about digging down to expose all the perfection you hide inside. By allowing yourself to go through the work, you will eventually become everything that you came here to be.

The Mast

Beyond all that you know, there is fear. As you peer into the depths of the sea, you may be afraid of what you can't see. You stand there on your sinking ship, clinging to the mast as if it is all that keeps you from certain death. What you don't understand is that there is no fear in the unknown.

It is not in holding on, that you will find your most beautiful treasures, it is in letting go. Your ship carried you through many storms and battles but it is only one ship on a vast sea.

As you look out at the ocean, see it in a different light. See the gentleness of the waves as they reach to caress your skin. Look to the moon as it casts a glittered light on the quiet ripples of the sea. See the North Star, always present to guide you. Now look closely, and see the small vessel floating on the water and know that you can let go of the sinking ship.

Do not hold on in fear. Take a huge breath and release your hold. Allow yourself to step out in faith and know that the sea will always catch you and carry you to safety. There is such peace in the process of letting go of control. That is where the miracles of this lifetime are found.

So it is with life. We cling so tightly to what we know that we hold ourselves back from becoming everything we can become. Lifetime after lifetime we come here, seeking completion in our own perfection, and so often, we forget that we are so much greater than what is held within the confines of our own humanity. We cling to life as if this is all we will ever have, and it is not until it is over, that we remember the vastness of who we really are.

Once again, you have come. Your soul whispers through the storms, "Can you remember who you are, or are you destined to repeat? There is nothing to fear in letting go, for it is in this release that you will finally remember your own magnificence.

Visualize yourself falling into the ocean. The water is not harsh. It is warm and gentle. It carries you gently on its waves. A tiny blue dragonfly lands on our big toe for a rest. For a while, be like the dragonfly and just rest.

Captain's Log: The Mast

Everything is different. We are in a huge shift and the old ways of doing things are changing to meet a new energy.

Each one of us has a choice to make. We can hold on to that old energy for dear life, or we can let go and allow a new energy to change everything we once believed.

Many of us are old souls and feel content right where we are, but we can't keep up with this new shift unless we're willing to change the way we think. As we feel the shift, we feel as if the eggshell that is protecting us is breaking and falling away. We desperately try to hold on, and pull all of the pieces back together again. When we give up the struggle, we suddenly realize that in

14

letting the shell fall away, we can finally see the beautiful new light that is shining through what used to be darkness.

This is when we find that there's a new energy, a new way of doing things. We find new gifts and we realize that our hearts are wide open to one another. Suddenly, the way we view relationships changes, and we know that we are much more connected than we have been led to believe. Those old beliefs about how we age, about how we heal, how we educate our children, they all begin to shift.

This is not a time to sit around and be afraid, it is a time to just lay it all down. Lay down everything you have learned, everything you believe, everything you hold onto so tightly, and realize when you let go of all of that baggage, you make room for the new.

Every day you'll be amazed what you're capable of. You aren't losing anything by letting go, but you will be overjoyed at what you will gain.

The Plank

The captain stood on the shore and silently watched as the ship sailed out to sea. A piece of her heart would always sail on that ship but she knew it was time to let it go.

Quietly, she dropped her eyes to the sand beneath her. She saw her footprints in the sand, leading from the ocean water to where she now stood alone.

Letting go was not something she was good at but she was learning that in letting go, she could begin again. She did not turn back to watch the ship leave the horizon. That chapter was over and she was ready to turn the page.

She took off her pirate boots and left them sitting there in the fading light. She began to walk and as she did, little by little, she dropped the pieces of her past.

She held her sword in her hands. The weight of it, now, just a burden that slowed her down. She dropped it in the sand. She would no longer need it to survive.

She looked back and saw how those things that seemed so important not so long ago, now held nothing but sorrow and she was glad to walk away.

She turned back to the new path before her. The setting sun lit the path in soft glowing light. Now unburdened from the past, her steps grew lighter, her heart lit up with unexpected joy and she smiled.

There comes a time for each one of us when we simply know that a chapter is complete. There is a restless feeling as if we need to let go of the past and begin again. There is great strength in letting go of the old and stepping forward into a brand-new life.

Learning to walk the plank and step out into the unknown is no longer scary when you know that you are never alone, or that nothing happens without a purpose and a plan. We don't have to know what awaits us as we take that first big step, we only need to remember that this life is meant to be an adventure. In those moments when we are forced to face the unknown, we can stand strong and confident in our own power and know that we have all of the tools we need to make it safely to the shore.

Captain's Log: The Plank

Each one of us comes to this planet seeking our own buried treasure. With bright-eyed wonder, the tendrils of curiosity reach out and create clues that will help us along the way. As children, we daydream, as we create our own little worlds of wonder and magic and then we are taught to live in the reality that dreams are not real and that life requires pain and hardship.

What if I told you that those daydreams are now ready to become your reality? What if I told you that it is time to let go of that old way of thinking, lay it all down and realize, that we are no longer required to live in a world of darkness?

This world is filled with people who will never realize their own greatness. They are content to go through life each day as if it is only a chore that needs to be completed before they can go on to their reward. You are different. You are a seeker of buried treasures. You carry a light within you that is so bright that you can see past the false realities to the place where all of your dreams will come true.

I will not tell you that this is an easy process. It requires hard work and bravery. It requires that you be willing to drop all of those labels and old habits that only serve to hold you back, in order to see in yourself, the greatness that you are.

In the process of letting go, there will be times that you will feel alone as you walk away from those relationships and situations, that no longer serve you. The loneliness will soon lift as you come fully into the awareness that all around you are golden cords that connect you to a spiritual team that is always available to guide and protect you. One by one you will discover new members of your tribe that have also come to experience this new paradigm. Nothing is ever removed from your life without an even greater replacement to fill the void.

You are one of the seekers that came here to experience this world in an entirely new light. This is not the first time you have come here and it will very likely not be your last. This time is different. In this new shift for this planet, new abilities are unfolding. It is a time for each soul to make a choice. We can choose to let go of the old ways, and ride this new wave of light, or we can step back into the ways of the past and join the masses of discontent.

The choice is yours. As you read this book, treat it as a journey of self-discovery. Allow the words to dig down deep, back to that small child who believed that anything was possible. Find that child that spent hours dreaming of a magical life and realize that in this new light, you truly are capable of creating your dreams. All it requires is that you let go of the person that was taught to live in a painful reality, and remember the limitless being that you really are.

The Shovel

In every pirate lies the heart of a child. Do you know what happens when you finally dig down deep enough to find and heal your inner child? That is the day when you finally feel completely secure in who you really are. There is an overwhelming peace in knowing that you are loved beyond measure, that not a single second goes by, when you are ever left alone on the savage seas.

Suddenly you are that tiny child curled up in the lap of love. This is when you finally let go of the illusion of separation, and you remember that no matter what horrors you may have gone through in your life as a pirate, they no longer hold any power over you. Like a child waking up from a nightmare, you realize that you are safe and wrapped in the arms of love.

Happiness lies in letting go and digging down deep, until we can finally find the treasure buried within. It isn't always easy. The process takes work and perseverance, but with every layer of damage that we peel away, comes the gift of love beyond measure.

Every passing day brings more joy, until one day you will wake up and realize that you are there. Suddenly, you just know that the magic you believed in as a small child is real. You finally realize that, you are the magic, and that this life is nothing less than purely miraculous.

The Captain's Log: The Shovel

Who were you when you were very young? Think back to those days when you spent hours creating your own little world of magic under a fort made of blankets. You were the king or queen of your kingdom, that was filled with unicorns, dragons, and pirate ships.

Your vision was wide open and in those times when you were alone, you felt a presence there with you. In those moments, you simply went within yourself and pulled out someone to play with.

Was that just imagination or was that imaginary friend really there?

This is where you need to change what you may have been taught. Of course that imaginary friend was real and still is. We are all surrounded by angels, spirit guides, and loved ones. They come from within our hearts and we are never without them.

Even when you stopped believing in them, they stayed with you. They quietly guide and comfort you and they wait. They wait for you to wake up from your amnesia and remember them. They long to communicate with you and to shower you with amazing gifts.

Can you remember the child within you who just knew he could fly? Do you remember when you used to that look into the woods and you saw fairies dancing through the trees, or dragons flying in the sky? That is still you. Somewhere inside of you, your inner child still lives.

Nurture your child. Allow your child to transport you back into the world of magic where nothing is impossible. When you do this, you will discover that the ability to create the world of your dreams lies within you. Even the moon and stars will be within your reach. The trick to becoming all that you can be truly is that simple.

The Quill

I see a pirate sitting in his cabin, quietly planning his voyage out on the high seas. As he dips his quill in to the ink, and applies it to the parchment, he visualizes the places he will go. There is excitement in every twist and turn of the quill.

He visualizes deep blue seas, castles, and hidden treasures. He is the commander of his vessel and he stands with confidence, unafraid of the unknown.

Like that pirate, each of us is an author, and with every moment that we live, we are quietly pressing the pen to the paper as we add new pages to the story of our lives. Something beautiful happens when we finally figure out that the choices are ours, and that we are the ones holding the quill.

We are not tiny lifeboats just being tossed around on the waves. We are each commanders of the lives that we choose to live. It is time to let go of the belief that you have no power over your circumstances.

Creating the life of your dreams requires intent and imagination. It requires you to look into the mirror and find the love that you long for, in your own reflection. It requires daydreams and laughter and joy.

It is time to let go of the idea that you are only here to suffer or that you are a helpless pawn. Your job is not difficult and your only sacrifice will be in letting go of those beliefs that no longer serve you. Tear those pages out of your story book and begin again. Go within yourself and begin to create a brand-new story that is filled with adventure on the high seas.

Put your quill to the parchment and write yourself into the most beautiful creation that your imagination will allow. You are the only person who can keep you from living the life of your dreams so start writing your adventure, pirate. You are a masterpiece in the making.

Captain's Log: The Quill

As I look back, I can see that my life has been one big treasure map. Along the paths of my life, there were clues, signs and symbols, to lead me on my way. I realize now, that I was never alone, not even in my darkest moments.

As I sit here writing down those things that I was drawn to, I see the connections, the perfection of a plan that was laid out long before I began this journey.

We can never begin to imagine the magnificence of who we truly are, until we until we are willing let go of false belief and self-doubt. It is in letting go of all negative baggage that we make room for a beautiful expansion that will open us up to the world of our dreams.

Most humans will not discover their own brilliance while they inhabit their human bodies, but there are a few who are brave enough to have a taste of their true identities. I am thankful to be one of those seekers, who refuses to see myself through the limitations of the human mind.

The greatest realization comes in simply letting go. We can never fully become who we really are until we are willing to let go of who we have been taught that we are. It is in this gentle release, that our eyes are finally opened up to the realization that God does not hide somewhere high in the clouds. Yes, there is a God, and he lives within each one of us.

Who are we then to feel small and insignificant? Do you believe that the creator of the heavens and the earth is tiny and weak? No, you do not. So, then, it is only logical that if God lies within you, and God is powerful, then you are powerful.

You are a creator of life and miracles. You are a spark of God, and you are capable of manifesting the life of your dreams. Open the door to your imagination and daydream, doodle and create. Set your intention on your creation, and just watch as the Universe throws open the doors and windows to your dreams.

As I become more accustomed to the knowing of who I really am, I find that everything is different. The world of my dreams is like a fairytale. Every walk in the woods is like a trip to wonderland. Every sunset, like a clear view of Heaven and every person that I see is like a character out of a favorite storybook.

The Crew

This voyage can seem long and tiring. There are days when it feels like a pirate carries the weight of the world. The seas are rough, and many times he longs for dry land. It is in those moments when he needs his crew.

There is never a time when **you** are required to fight the storms alone. No matter how rough the seas may get, if you turn to your crew, they are always there to help steer your ship to a safe port in the storm.

Life is not always easy for lightworkers . There are those days that our highly sensitive souls take on too much water. As we get pulled under the seas, it can be difficult to fight back up to the surface for a breath of fresh air.

No matter how you may feel, you are never alone. Wherever your ship takes you, there is always a mate to pick you up when you are down, or help you find your direction when you feel lost. Many times you may think that you can stay afloat all on your own, but try to remember, your crew is always happy to throw you a life preserver when you need one.

We can't always be the hero. There always will be those days when we have to allow ourselves to be pulled back up from the depths of the sea. Learn to trust your mates and they will never let you down.

Captain's Log: The Crew

Each one of us came here with a team. We have never been alone, even in those darkest times when all we could find was despair. There always has been that still, small voice whispering to us that we are not alone, and that we are so loved.

Take time every day to realize that you are engulfed by the love of your very own spiritual team. They always **are** there, ready to comfort and protect. There is only one thing that stops them. That is you and your own free will. Do not expect them to fly in and rescue you unless you ask. It is not that they don't want to. They long to give you peace, love, joy, and protection, but you are the boss. They can't help you unless you ask.

As you create space for them in your life, as you learn to enjoy their presence, you will begin to finally feel the love that has always been there for you. Do not be afraid to call on them. They are not limited by time or space. They never look at you as if you are a burden. They are pure love and they long to shower you in their beautiful light.

As you practice getting to know your team, you will begin to transform. You will begin to know each one of them by the way that they feel. It is perfectly okay to ask questions, be playful, laugh, and enjoy the feeling of their presence.

Paul tells the story of a time when he wanted to be sure that the messages he was receiving were from his own team and not some dark entity who was trying to fool him. He sat there in a quiet room, and he asked, "How do I know this is you?" He felt someone touch his head. He asked again and he felt a twitch in his lip. When he asked a third time, he felt a touch on the back of his arm. The fourth time he asked, he felt a tickle in the center of his back that became so intense that he fell on the floor laughing and yelled out, "Okay, okay, I will never ask again!"

This is how loved we are. We can choose to walk this Earth feeling alone, or we can choose to reach out to the team that surrounds us. We can come at this as a small child who is filled with wonder. We can enjoy the presence of God, of Jesus, of Ascended Masters and Archangels.

Yes, you **are** really that special. You chose to come here. You are fulfilling an important mission and because of that, you have a team that is always available to help you get through it. They know that you are on the front line of battle, and when you allow them in, you will find that they are always there just waiting for your command. You are never alone.

Treasure Map

My life is a fairy tale and I am constantly putting words to the pages as I create a life that is filled with magic. Every day, we are creating a story for ourselves. We have the choice of living a nightmare or a fairy tale. When we look around, we can see bugs that bite, or tiny fairies dancing through the trees. We look to the clouds and we see a storm brewing, or we can see dragons spreading their wings and flying across the sky. We are powerful creators. What story are you creating for yourself today?

When we were children, our imaginations ran free. We believed in anything and everything. We dreamed of swashbuckling pirates out on the open sea, fighting sea monsters, and burying treasure on deserted islands. We longed to find our own treasure maps that would lead us to a trunk full of treasure. We still believed that everyone would eventually see their own happy ending.

Then, the world kicked in and tried to tell us to get our heads out of the clouds. "Stop using your imagination. That won't get you anywhere." We got in trouble for daydreaming, for doodling, for spending time creating our own imaginary kingdoms to run to, when we needed an escape from a painful world.

Consider your imagination as your treasure map. You can't ever fully attain your highest potential while you deny yourself your imagination. We each have a conscious mind and a subconscious mind. Those two avenues are constantly congested with traffic. They are busy and when we spend all of our time there, we find ourselves frustrated and confused. We lose the wind from our sails.

Imagination is the third option. Imagination is what opens us up to truly seeing who we really are and what we are capable of achieving. When you meditate, don't be afraid of letting your imagination take the front seat and just see where it takes you. Manifesting is all about letting go of what you have been told is impossible. It is the realization that if you can imagine something clearly enough, you can create it.

Many use the word visualization, instead of imagination but they are one in the same. Allow yourself to fall into the world of fairytale land. See yourself in the happiest place you can imagine. No matter what your outside circumstances may be, somewhere inside of you, is that small child who still believes in dragons, and happy endings.

Allow yourself to be that child again. See yourself as a swash-buckling pirate that can slay sea monsters or save the damsel in distress. Be your favorite super hero. You really are you know. You are a super hero and all of those voices in your head that tell you you are anything less, let them go and walk away.

It is when we dig down in and find our inner children, that we discover how simple this life is supposed to be. We are not here to suffer, struggle and fight. Like the small child, we simply need to "know" that we are wrapped up in the arms of love, that no dream is impossible and that we are worthy of living a life that is filled with magic.

Captain's Log: Treasure Map

Imagination combined with intention create the golden key to the door of spirituality and manifestation

There is a new energy on this Earth and with that energy comes a freedom like we have never known. We need to let go of the old ways of doing things.

This planet has gone through a major shift and the ability to create the life of your dreams is right there within your reach. This is the greatest lesson I can teach you. You must stop looking at yourself as tiny and insignificant. Inside of you lies the spark of God, and with that, the power to create in ways that you never have known before.

The magical formula is so simple that most will refuse to believe, but if you are drawn to this book, it is because you are different. This is why you are here. Manifestation only requires a few main ingredients.

The first ingredient is self-love. Take the time to look in your mirror every day and fall in love with the person who is looking back at you. Love yourself in the way that you wish to be loved. It seems so easy for empaths to give great love to others, and yet, so often, we forget that we deserve that same love.

Spend time thinking about those things that bring you joy. Create a plan for your own happiness and remind yourself daily that you deserve to be blissfully happy. There is great power in self-love.

The second ingredient is imagination. Can you remember what you were like as a child before you were taught to stop using your imagination? Sitting at your desk at school, you would daydream and create entire kingdoms. Dragons would fly around the room, as you would save the damsel in distress.

In your dreams there were no thoughts of limitation or scarcity. You simply allowed your imagination to fly free. Forget all of the times you were told to grow up and stop daydreaming. In order to come completely into your own power, you must use your imagination to open up your ability to see the changes you want, even before they become a reality.

The third ingredient is your intent. As you create your dreams through your imagination, you must then set your intention on what you wish to manifest into your reality. This is only a matter of truly knowing what it is that you want, and believing in your own ability to create it. You may begin small, but, as you realize your own power to manifest, you will find that your abilities grow. Soon, you will be living a life that you never dreamed possible.

The icing on the cake is gratitude. Having a grateful heart, opens the door to greater opportunities to receive. It is like a sign to the Universe that you are always open to accept more abundance into your life.

Think about it. You can create the life you have always longed for. You are mighty. You are magic. As you let go of the belief that you are only a pawn, and realize that you are the captain of your own ship, you will begin to feel the ease in life. Amazing things will happen and you will sit and smile as you realize that you made it. You came here to experience this, and you have arrived.

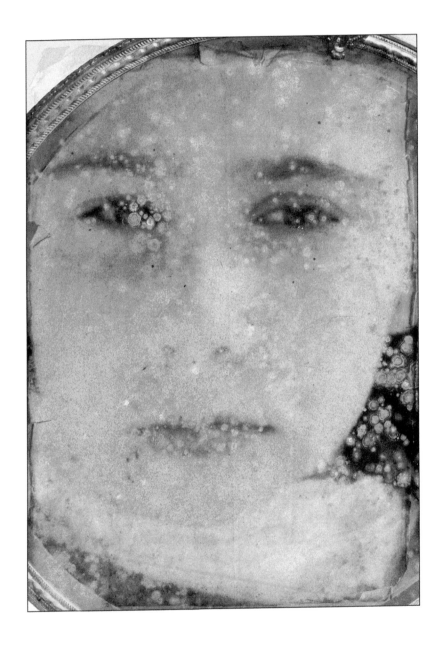

The Mirror

Her trunk was full of treasures and it all sparkled like glitter in the sunlight. The captain reached in and held each little pearl, and every piece of gold, and she smiled with the memories they each held.

As she laid each piece aside, her hand landed on an old hand mirror. She wondered why this old piece was among so many treasures.

She held it up to her face and viewed the girl shining back. She was startled a bit at what she saw. This was not the pirate she had become. What she saw was a fresh face with bright eyes and a pretty smile. The years of pain had melted away to reveal the child **who** had been buried deep within.

She barely recognized the girl, and yet in her heart she knew the truth. That old hardened pirate was not who she really was. That was only a facade that hid her beautiful heart. The reflection in the mirror showed her true self, the one that she was, before the world had stolen her innocence. Now, as she peered into the clear shining eyes looking back at her, she smiled.

The old mirror in her hands was not just junk, amid treasure at all. This mirror was the window to her soul, and by looking into it, she felt renewed and alive with the knowledge that the years of pain and suffering had not stolen her true beauty at all. That girl was still there, buried deep within, just waiting to be brought back up into the sunlight and allowed to shine.

Captain's Log: The Mirror

When you look upon yourself, what do you see? Do you see the scars, wrinkles and damage you carry from lifetimes upon the Earth? Do you only see your faults?

It is time to shed that old reality that you have wrapped yourself in. Within you, there is a light that shines so brightly that rainbows shoot out of your soul.

If you could only see a tiny piece of your own magnificence, you would never doubt yourself again. You are a miracle, all wrapped up in human form. What you see as you look in your mirror is only the wrapping paper. That is not the gift.

Take the time each day, to give yourself a smile. Give yourself the love that you long for.

We live in a world that takes so much from us. It is time that you learn how to fill yourself back up with all the love you deserve.

Wrap yourself in a warm hug and look past the physical faults until all you see is the diamond that you are, perfect, multifaceted, and magnificently made.

The Compass

The boy stood on the shore and looked out over the vast ocean. Through his eyes, everything was alive. The waves were mighty sea monsters. He saw their many tentacles and deep green eyes as they wrapped themselves around ships and pulled them in all directions.

He heard the seagull laugh at the dolphins as they played hide and seek in the coral.

The sea turtles gathered to tell ancient stories about the creation of the blue moon, as the sun came close to listen and cast a gentle red flame over the sea.

Lost in his world of imagination, the boy did not notice as his father walked up behind him. The man spoke not a word as he gently reached for the boy's hand and laid in it a golden compass and then quietly walked away.

The boy felt the weight of the object and his heart swelled. In that simple action his father had set him free. This was the gift he had longed for. He lowered his eyes and looked at the compass as a tear rolled gently down his face. He was filled with excitement and sadness as the emotions swirled into a small whirlpool in his soul.

It was time to leave the safety of his peaceful home. He had felt the winds of change and this came as no surprise, but still there was a fleeting sense of loss.

He knew that he had a beautiful mission but in accepting this adventure, he would have to step out into the darkness of the sea.

The weight of that small compass suddenly reminded him of his dreams. He knew he could not remain in this safe port forever. He was not made that way. His heart was too big, his courage, too strong. A smile touched his cheeks as joy filled his soul.

It was time to breathe life into his daydreams. Soon the world would see a man where this boy once stood. With every turn of his compass, he would breathe light into the darkness, for this was the mission he had chosen.

With a new confidence, he stepped into the sea. He knew that his compass would guide him to wherever he needed to be, and when his mission was complete, it would bring him home again. He had nothing to fear. He was at peace.

Captain's Log: The Compass

Think of meditation as the most amazing compass. Meditation is not only going to point you in the right direction, it is also going to push the wind into your sails and blow you right to the island where your treasure awaits.

Now, relax and let me tell you a little story about meditation. When you were a small child, you knew how to meditate. Think of yourself in school. The teacher is teaching a very boring lesson.

40

Your mind shuts down and you drift off to another place, a magical place. You no longer hear the noise around you and for just a little while, you feel light and free. That was meditation. You were doing what comes naturally, but you very likely got in trouble for doing it, so you stopped, and you decided it was a bad thing. We come to this planet perfectly equipped with the tools we need and then, those tools get taught out of us.

Take a walk in the woods and let go of the worries of the day. Set them aside and just allow yourself to bask in the smells, sounds, and sights around you. Put in your earbuds and play music that makes your heart smile. Lay your head back and just allow it to fill your soul. Go to the beach and close your eyes, as you inhale the salty air, and listen to the waves hit the shore. Get out your colored pencils and an art pad and doodle and create. Write yourself a fairytale and get lost in it. Meditation happens anytime we shut down the brain and allow our spirits to fly. It isn't work and it isn't scary. It is simply taking the time to go back to being that child that got lost in a daydream.

Meditation allows us to be the wind in our own sails. Like the compass, it points us in the direction we long to go. It will always lead you to the most amazing treasures.

The Anchor

You are not just any pirate. You are a pirate king or queen. You hold treasures beyond measure. You have sorted through them and gathered them and you have filled many trunks.

Your only problem is that you have dropped your anchor and it is holding you back. It is time to pull up your anchor to allow your ship to glide freely through the sea.

How many times have you called out to God to show you the way to your treasure and then something happened to push your ship to a distant shore? Often the winds went still and your ship floated helplessly on open seas and you feared that you may never find your way.

The truth is, most of us look at this life the wrong way. We play the victim as the wind and waves take us through life. The only way we can find our treasure is to look at all of life's adventures as filled with purpose.

This is how we find all of that buried treasure we are seeking. We must stop playing the role of victim and realize that everything that happens in this life is nothing more than an experience. Often the most painful experiences are the ones that serve the greatest purpose.

You are a powerful creator. You have the power to change all that is negative in your life, but you must change the way you are seeing your experiences. With only your imagination and intent you have the ability to change your ship's direction. Your treasure lies within you. Nothing holds you back from it but your own negative emotions and beliefs. Every day, take the time to pull up your anchor, and allow your ship to flow freely through the water.

The most important thing you will ever learn is that this life does not require you to be in complete control. When you finally learn to pull up the anchor and let go, you will find that it isn't as important to just find your treasure, as it is to enjoy the journey along the way.

The Captain's Log: The Anchor

Life is not supposed to be constantly comfortable. It is those discomforts that push us to step out into the unknown. That is where we find that we aren't fully living until we grab on to those fears that have been holding us back and then use them to launch us into the greatest adventures we will ever know.

Learn to look at your fears and discomforts as just something that is meant to push you out of your comfort zone. If life was always comfortable, we would have no reason to come here in the first place. Every single experience that we have has meaning and purpose. When we let go of the idea that we are helpless victims and realize that we each have unlimited power, we will realize that there is no reason to hold ourselves back.

Begin a practice of letting go of your fears. Step out boldly with confidence, into the unknown. Even when you can't see the whole picture, it is still better to take a chance, than it is to just sit still in fear. You aren't going to fall off into the unknown. There will always be a safe place to land.

This life is meant to be lived to the fullest. The unknown isn't so scary once you allow yourself to just let go and fall into it. You are brave and powerful. Pull up your anchor and allow yourself to live the greatest adventure you have ever known.

Bottle of Rum

What do you think of when you picture a ship full of pirates? I see the child like imagination version of silly songs, practical jokes and loud laughter. In that version, I can truly say that it is a pirate's life for me.

Laughter comes as naturally to us as breathing. Every baby has that moment when they suddenly find their belly laugh and it sounds like heavenly music to our ears.

Many times, as lightworkers and empaths, we care so deeply about saving the world that we forget that this life is meant to be filled with joyful laughter. Laughter is the greatest way to spread joy to a world that seems way too serious. It is in our laughter that we spread healing.

Like magical fairydust, laughter fills a room with smiles, it is so contagious. Laughter is the most beautiful way to lift the vibration of the planet.

Get out there and enjoy your silly inner pirate today. Enjoy the gift of laughter and spread it everywhere you go.

Captains Log: Bottle of Rum

Being a lightworker, does not require us to be serious all of the time. Actually, it is quite the opposite. As you get to know your own team, don't be afraid to develop a closer relationship with them. They do not judge you no matter what you say or do. They only love.

So often, I find that when the Ascended Masters enter the room, they bring messages like, "Lighten up! It is only life!" They are constantly trying to remind us that we did not come here to be miserable. We came into this lifetime to find joy and what better way to find joy than through laughter?

The Crow's Nest

Standing on the deck, the captain felt overwhelmed. The damage from the storm the night before had created havoc. He glanced around at his crew, asleep right where they had collapsed out of exhaustion. The storm had been fierce and many times, they feared that they would pulled to the bottom of the sea.

Now, in the bright morning sun, the captain was overwhelmed with the damage he saw. Sails were torn and some were missing after being swept away in a gale of wind. There was water in the lower deck. The galley floor was covered in pots and pans, rotting vegetables, flour and a substance that he had not been able to identify.

Gingerly, the captain stepped over his sleeping mates as he made his way to the center of the ship. He laid his hands on the ladder and began to climb. Step by step, he felt the gentle release of the pressure on his chest. As he reached the Crow's nest he rested. He closed his eyes and he inhaled the fresh salty air.

He heard the sound of wings and looked up to find a large black crow had settled in on the ropes nearby. In the eyes of the bird, the captain saw peace. This bird had survived a storm so strong that it should have been blown into the sea and yet it was fine. Again, there was a release of pressure from the Captain's chest. He looked down at his crew and ship from up above it all, and suddenly, a wave of gratitude swept over him. Like the crow, he and his crew had survived. Not one man had been washed overboard. The ship was sound and it had carried them safely to a calm port.

As his heart filled with the realization of all that remained, the captain felt at peace. The worries washed away and were replaced with the knowing that all was well. The crew would soon awaken and the clean up would begin. Soon the ship would be back to its original splendor.

Looking down at his world from this new perspective had changed worry to peace. He was alive. His crew was alive. The ship still held the promise of adventure on the high seas. Like the crow, there was peace in the Captain's eyes as gratitude filled him and he found rest.

Sea Legs

Pirates spend months at sea. It doesn't take them long to learn to roll with the wind and the waves. They train their legs to bend and their feet to hold steady no matter how much the ship may sway.

Then comes the day when they reach their island where their treasure is buried, and as their feet hit solid ground, they find it difficult to walk without falling down. The ground feels foreign to them, and they often trip over their own feet. It takes time to retrain their legs to stand on solid ground.

I am sure that we have all developed a set of sea legs. Since the very beginning of our lives, we have each learned to roll with the wind and the waves. As children, we learned to bend so that we wouldn't break. We learned to build up walls around ourselves to protect against the storms.

Those walls may have been necessary when we were small, but they no longer **are** needed. We have come to our safe port and it is time to learn to walk on solid ground. It is tempting to keep our walls up. The problem with this is that those walls keep us from our dreams. Everything we want in life stands on the other side of those walls.

Always remember to be gentle with yourself. Your inner child is often afraid to let go of the walls that hold you back. Step lightly and carefully as if you just stepped off of your ship. Feel the ground beneath you, and allow yourself the time to become steadier with every step you take.

Accept the fact that you will trip and fall a few times along the way. You are always protected, so just allow yourself to fall gently to the ground and rest until you feel strong again.

You can't mess this up. There is no wrong way to get back to who you really are, except to let fear stop you from trying.

The Ship

The captain stood at his wheel as he surveyed the shallow waters. The storm had carried his ship into a hazardous bay where large rocks jutted out of the water. He was thankful that his ship was still afloat because as he looked at the sharp rocks, he knew that his ship had been guided to rest in this place by a hand larger than his own.

Now in the daylight, he could see the dangers all around, and he could not find a clear path back out to the sea. He closed his eyes in exhaustion and rested for a moment.

As he found peace, he knew the answer he had been seeking. He was going to have to get out of this danger, in the same way he got in. The night before, all was dark. He could not see the dangers and yet, somehow, his ship made it to safety.

He realized that it was only his fear that was holding him back. He would have to let go of all his fears to find his way out. The captain looked out at his crew, as they worked to shine their beloved ship. His heart swelled with love as he listened to their laughter. He had chosen this crew carefully, and he had grown quite fond of each one of them.

He then looked at his parrot and remembered how this bird had stayed there on his shoulder through all of life's storms. Again, he felt love.

His ship gleamed in the sunlight. The wood had a special creak to it that comforted him and gave him peace on those nights he struggled to sleep. He loved this ship.

As the captain continued to focus on everything that was good, and that brought him love, he released any fears that may have been holding him back. With the anchor pulled up, he noticed that the ship has been quietly moving through the bay as if, tiptoeing through the dangers, while he was busy focusing on love.

He looked behind him at all of the sharp rocks that the ship had already cleared, and he knew that all was well. No matter what dangers **were** ahead, he knew that by letting go of his fear, and focusing on love, he would glide through safely and confidence.

Life at sea can be scary and fraught with dangers, but we can always weather the storms when we turn away from fear, and focus on love.

Love will always steer us in the direction that we need to go. It never fails.

Captain's Log: The Ship

Letting go of fear is what turns the tide from hardship to joy. In all things, we have the choice to react out of love or out of fear.

Consider the choices you have made in your life. Remember that there truly are no wrong choices but every choice you have made has led you to a different destination.

Now as you look back, can you remember how you felt as you considered your decisions? Did you react out of fear or did you react out of love?

We truly are magnets. We get back what we put out. Fear will bring fear along with a pile of other negative emotions and the end results will likely not be what you were hoping for.

Love brings love. It can do nothing less. This response requires practice. From the time we were very young, we were programmed to survive. Like a fawn that is taught to run in fear, we were taught the same. What if you wake up to the idea that there truly is nothing to be afraid of. You are not that tiny fawn. You are a fierce lion. Within you lies more strength than you have ever realized.

In those moments where a decision needs to be made, take the time to meditate on **it**. Look deeply within your heart and decide what is holding you back. Are you afraid to take that first big step?

What if you realized that all that lies below in the darkness is a gentle stream that will cushion your fall? What if you realized that you are the commander of your ship and that by taking fear out of the equation, all that is left is love, and love will always catch you when you fall.

Pirate Hat

D o you remember when you used to love to play in the dirt? Every small child is drawn to nature. It doesn't matter what the weather looks like to a five-year-old. Rain blesses them with puddles and mud. Snow is the perfect building material for a magnificent fort. The summer sun brings the opportunity sand-castles and swimming in the lake, and the fall brings crisp cool air and piles of leaves to play in.

With your pirate hat in place for protection, it is time to remember your natural instinct for the Earth's ability to ground you. These days we are constantly surrounded by electronics, artificial lights, and pavement. Empaths are especially sensitive to the ravages of what we like to call progress.

Always, there is a small voice inside you that cries out to stick your feet in the dirt. Listen to that voice. Sit right down in the grass and take off your shoes. Allow the Earth to infuse you with the most beautiful energy that only she can offer.

Lay out under a full moon or walk amid the trees. Slow down and enjoy the sunrises and the sunsets.

You came to this planet knowing how to ground yourself. Do you remember who you were before you decided to grow up? It is time to remember the joy of being totally covered in mud again. There is no shame in making mud pies.

Play in the rain with reckless abandon. Take off your shoes and let the mud squish between your toes. Life is meant to be disorderly, and dirty, and full of spontaneous merrymaking.

Captain's Log: The Pirate Hat

Being energy sensitive is beautiful and painful all wrapped up in one package. It is growing up feeling sick most of the time or exhausted and not really knowing why.

Not only do we suffer from picking up the illnesses and emotions of others, but we also suffer from the environments that we live in. Artificial lighting, processed foods, pavement, chemicals, strong smells, particulates in the air, and extreme heat or cold, can cause severe reactions.

Often, we will feel the stress through anxiety or allergies, chronic fatigue, or illness. Nature has a way of healing and renewing our ability to exist in a world that feels like it is out to get us.

Look around you. Your environment is constantly having an effect on you, whether that **is** good or bad. It is important to take time to allow nature to renew your strength. By taking off your shoes and walking in the grass or on a beach, you are allowing yourself to become grounded and connected to the Earth.

Being grounded brings a natural peace and comfort to an empath. As you spend more time feeling the healing and regenerating power of the Earth, you will find it is easier to cope with the stresses this life throws at you. So, take off your shoes, get out there and enjoy all of the gifts that nature has to offer you.

The Skeleton Keys

The captain stood on the deck of the ship and looked at the horizon. There would be no more hiding treasure for this pirate, no more coveting gold. He reached to pick up the golden ring of skeleton keys. The wind blew and forced the keys to chime, as if to serve as a wake-up call to the sleeping crew.

One by one they awoke, and as they looked to the captain, they saw the change. No longer was this the captain that they knew. His doubts and fears seemed replaced with strength and knowledge. He stood tall in self- confidence and determination. They were silenced into a new respect as they awaited his command.

He reached **into** his pocket and pulled out the map. This was not just any map. This map showed the way to the most amazing treasures anyone had ever seen. These were treasures that had been buried through the lifetimes of many of his ancestors. Each previous generation, had hoped to be the one that would be called to use the map to find the treasures, but that call didn't come, until now.

The time had to be perfect. This captain was chosen. There he stood, a new light shining in his eyes. He would be the one to carry the keys to the treasures, so long buried, as they finally made their way back into the light.

He ordered the crew and they hoisted the sails. As they worked they sang and laughed with the joy of knowing that they too were chosen to be the ones that would support and aid the captain on his most important mission.

The wind picked up and filled the sails, as the ship hastily cut through the sea. With each creek of the wood, each lap of the waves, the ship itself seemed to tell the story of a new Earth, of peace, and the end of all battles

The captain pulled out his telescope and looked off to the horizon, "Land Ho" he yelled as the crew prepared the small boat that would carry them to shore. He took his shovel and dropped into the boat, silently preparing for the moment that was sure to come.

Finding the place of the X on his map, he began to dig. This would be his job as the crew stood back quietly watching. He would be the one to expose this beautiful treasure to the sun and he felt gratitude with every shovelful of sand. He was careful so as not to damage the pirate chest. It took time and patience, but he knew this job could not be rushed. With one final push, he felt the soft touch and heard the quiet thud of his shovel as it touched the chest. He dropped to his knees and began to clear away the sand with his hands. Carefully, he exposed the small chest and he lifted it out of the hole and set it gently on the beach.

The crew stood back, holding their breath. The king reached for his keys and held them in his hand. He knew by the energy which key he would need. He inserted it into the lock and heard the small click as it turned. Excitement built in his heart as the lid lifted up and exposed the treasure to the sun.

A million tiny rainbows shot forth from the diamond that lay within. The crew fell to their knees. This was a treasure unlike anything they had ever seen. They were each overcome with the energy they felt and they bowed their heads in reverence.

The captain reached into the chest and picked up the diamond. He felt the energy pulse up his arm, and into his heart and in that instant, he was transformed. No longer was he a pirate bearing the scars of battle. Here, now, he was changed into the mighty king that he came here to be. His sins were forgiven. His past was wiped away, and this was a new day. Today, he was brand new. Today, he would begin again.

No longer would he walk in darkness or bring pain. It was time for everything to change. He would continue to follow his map. Forever more, his days would be filled with finding perfect treasures, and bringing their light back into the world.

He, who was the holder of the keys, would work to dispel the darkness and bring the world back into perfect light.

The Parrot

There is a large brightly colored parrot on your shoulder. He is very good at repeating everything you say.

So often, we speak without realizing that everything we say is like magic. Our words are like spells as we weave this web that we call life.

As you stand there at the wheel of your ship, what will your parrot repeat today? Will the words that he bounces right back at you, calm the seas or bring about a mighty storm? Will he encourage you to create a more beautiful life, or will his words build a wall of fear around you?

Remember that your crew hears your parrot and they take action. You are a powerful captain and with every thought that you think, with every word that you speak, you have the ability to change your world.

What are you teaching your parrot today?

Captain's Log: The Parrot

Affirmations are a powerful tool. Like the parable of the parrot, you too have an echo response to your words and thoughts. Every word that you say holds power.

As you look upon yourself, remember that is is important to be kind. Your words affect your health and well-being. They affect your ability to manifest the life of your dreams. So be gentle with yourself.

Affirmations can be a powerful tool in your toolbox. Take the time to speak positive thoughts to yourself. Change your words from, "Why am I always getting sick?" To "I am thankful that I am able to heal." Change from, "I am broke." to "My needs are always met." You can say things like "I have unlimited resources." or "I am living the life of my dreams."

It takes practice to believe in what you can't yet see, but this is the best way to convince your ego that everything is perfect. It is the way that you shut down the worries and concerns that pull you into that lower vibration, and by doing so, you will manifest the life of your dreams even faster than you ever thought possible.

The Lantern

The world of a pirate can often seem like a very dark place. That is when it is important to remember that we each carry a bright lantern within us.

No matter how calm or how rough the seas may get, we must choose to pull out our lantern in order to claim our power over the elements around us.

The problem with most pirates is that they have forgotten that the lantern is always there to help them see more clearly.

As young pirates they were often taught to keep their lanterns hidden. They have forgotten what an amazing tool they were given.

Your lantern is as bright as the sun. This is the core of who you really are, and as you remember this blindingly beautiful light that you carry within you, your life will begin to shine more brightly.

As you meditate, find that inner light and imagine that light expanding so big and bright that it pops right out of your body and fills the room, nine feet in every direction. This creates a safe bubble for healing and protection. If we can imagine this bubble wrapped in angelic purple, blue, and lavender light, we are then free to imagine ourselves perfectly wrapped up and protected against the outside forces that might harm us.

Safe in this bubble, you become free to get lost in your own beautiful daydream. This is the time to let your imagination soar.

Where do you wish to be? Will you fly through the stars to a brand-new galaxy, or imagine yourself in a field full of daisies? Are you sitting on top of mountain, or are you a pirate out at sea?

The most important thing that we need to remember is that within each one of us lies a spark of God. This light you pull out of your center, is your God light. It is your inner power. When you pull that light out, you are remembering that God does not hide somewhere out there in the clouds. God is within you. You are God.

Each one of us is busily creating the world around us with our every thought, word and action, whether good or bad. By remembering to use your lantern to see in the darkness, you are allowing your very own spark of God to fly free to create a more beautiful reality.

It takes practice and perseverance, but don't stop uncovering your lantern. Pull it out often and let your light shine brightly until you create the paradise of your dreams.

Captain's Log: The Lantern

Have you ever wondered how it is that God, the Arc Angels, Jesus or whoever else we choose to call on, seems to have the ability to be everywhere at the same time? The answer to that question is so simple that we often overlook it. It is because they come from within our own hearts.

God is purely the energy of love. He split that energy in to a billion pieces and gave each piece an identity. That is you and me and everyone else that you see.

In pulling that white light out from year heart, and expanding it to as big as you like, you aren't just pulling a piece of yourself out, you are pulling out that piece of you, that is God. That is the signal to your team that you are opening yourself up to everything that the Universe has to offer. You are ready for healing, for new abilities, for rewiring or upgrades and downloads of new information. You are saying that you are ready to be reminded of who you really are.

Are you ready to pull that treasure up out of the core of your own being? You aren't alone in this mission. We are many, and we are waking up together in order to bring this new way of living to each and every human being on the planet.

Get out your shovel, and start digging. Your treasure is right there waiting for you and this world needs you to claim it.

Sundial

I can see a pirate standing at the wheel, holding his sundial to the sky so that he can create his plans for his travel on the high seas.

Have you ever noticed that it isn't the arm of a sundial that tells the time, but the shadow of the arm? As I sit here contemplating life, I realize that it is in the shadows of my life that I find the most clarity

It is in those dark memories that the most lessons were learned. I realize now, as I look back, that every experience holds the ability to bring a higher state of awareness.

Something amazing happens as I rise above the emotions of my humanity. I can see my life laid out as a golden grid. Each line connects to the next as they stretch out to one another in perfect unison. There are no errors or mistakes. Each line is necessary in order for my creation to be complete.

This is the lesson of the sundial. A sundial will not work without both the sun and the shadow. We have the mistaken notion that we must always walk in the light. We feel the need for perfection, but without the shadows, we are missing the most important ingredient. We have no way to gauge our own progress without the darkness to balance the light.

Often, when we allow ourselves to rest in the shadows of our lives, we realize that those dark times were only there to lead us to an even greater light.

The Telescope

We can't always change the people, places and things that we have in our world. We can't change the way others think or feel. So, I give you this gift of a very special telescope. This telescope sees the world differently. It can only see things in a way that is for your highest good.

No matter who crosses your path, how they respond to you, or what may pop up to slow you down, remember to look at it all through this telescope, and you will see that it is all just an opportunity for you to grow and to shine even brighter.

Grab your trusty telescope and climb up to the crow's nest of your pirate ship and look at it all from this brand-new perspective. See it as the observer and understand that it is all just part of your adventure. You are not those pains and setbacks. You are so much more than that.

The Captain's Log: The Telescope

I am going to tell you a secret. You are much smarter than you have been led to believe.

For most of us, we believe that we are born as blank slates and then we learn everything from our parents or teachers, preachers or books. That isn't true. We are born knowing everything that we need to know.

It is in the present system of learning that we actually forget who we really are and what we are capable of. We teach our children to get their heads out of the clouds. We tell them to quiet their imaginations and we get angry when they daydream.

The greatest spiritual teachers understand that it isn't necessary to force any beliefs on anyone else. A good teacher knows that the key isn't in learning as much as it is in remembering, and that is how healing sessions work. It is a process of peeling away the false beliefs until we can dig down deep enough to remember who we really are.

True expansion comes when we revert back to that child **who** believed that anything was possible. Take a moment, and imagine that everything you have been taught is written on a large chalkboard. See yourself erasing it all away. Now you have a clean slate. Allow yourself to be the child. Pick up your chalk and doodle and create the life of your dreams.

As you learn to stomp through the mud puddles of life and dance like nobody's watching, you will begin to uncover your own truths. You will once again realize what you came to this planet already knowing, that life is meant to be filled with joy and that the only thing you truly came here to learn is that love conquers all.

The Pirate Chest

Not one of us came to this planet ill equipped. As I packed my pirate chest for a long voyage at sea, I carefully sorted through all of my different tools, and picked each one up and felt it's energy as I decided if it was a good fit for this voyage.

The first things I packed were my imagination, intuition, and sensitivity. Those are three things that I never leave home without. My mother walked into the room with a gift of love all wrapped up in perfect paper and placed it in my pirate chest. "Never forget this." she said. "When you feel lost at sea, open this package and remember that you are never too far away to feel my love." She quietly added a few gentle hugs to the chest before leaving the room.

I sifted some more and my hands fell on grief. "Should I?", I asked myself. The answer to this one wasn't so difficult while I was standing there bathed in love. Yes, I should, because this is one of those gifts that may hurt for a while, but has the ability to bring about a major transformation. I added it to the chest.

With that, I knew that I would need a little help to get through the pain, so I added "childlike spirit" to my chest. I remembered that having a healthy child living inside of me would bring joy after every storm.

I then chose humility so that I would never seem out of reach to anyone in need, but also added creativity so that I would have a way to shine.

I picked up loneliness and held it in my hand. This one would be difficult, but the experience would make me stronger, and with only a moment's hesitation, I laid it gently in my chest. For balance, I added a big smile. I knew that a smile would bring me the friendship that I would need to get through my darkest days.

As hardship touched my hand, I thought of leaving it behind. My chest was already quite full, but with hardship comes abundance in equal measure. They go hand in hand so they both joined my chest of treasures.

Then, before I forgot, I added fear. Why would I do that, you may ask? Because through fear we learn courage, and courage is always worth the fight.

When I realized that my chest was nearly full, I sprinkled tiny glitter filled stars over the top of all of it. With this, I knew, that no matter how dark the storm, if I looked up to the sky, the stars would always remind me that this life is only temporary, and that one day, when my work is complete, I will return to my own magical island on the other side of the moon.

The Captain's log; The Pirate Chest

Who were you before you became you? A year ago, I thought my life was ending, and in one way it was. That life that I was living was coming to a close, but my life was far from being over. Now, as I look back, I realize that it was all just a piece in the most beautiful puzzle that I have ever lived.

I have done this many times before. Chances are you have also. We sign on to play this game with the knowledge that we will forget everything we have ever learned. We agree to go through the same painful lessons again and again.

So often it cuts us to the very core of our being. Still, we come back. When asked if we will return once again, and pay the price to save others, we stand up proud and strong and ready to fight on the front lines.

So, I ask you again, who were you before you became you? Do you know? Can you look in the mirror and remember a perfectly devised plan? Can you remember that you came her so filled with love for humanity that you agreed to suffer for them? Can you look in the mirror and see the light that you carry within your heart that is capable of saving a world that is filled with darkness? Do you know that just by your very existence, you are succeeding magnificently?

Now, as I look back **on** my healing sessions with Paul, I can see how each one helped me to dig out another piece of myself that had been perfectly buried. It is hard work and often painful, but I have finally come to **the** day when I can see the diamond that I am inside.

Finally, strong, secure, and without fear, I step forward out of the role of victim and into the role of creator. This is who I came here to be. Who did you come here to be? Are you ready to find out?

The Captain's Quarters

The captain stepped into her quarters after a long, tiring day. She longed for the solitude, away from the noise of the crew. As she took off her hat and coat, she became aware of an odd feeling in her chest. Something felt off and the peace that she longed for was nowhere to be found.

She let her eyes wander through the cabin and fall on the things that used to give her joy. Everywhere she looked there were small treasures to catch the eye. She walked to her desk and lifted a small string of pearls. She held it gently and allowed the smooth feel of the pearls to caress her fingers. Memories filled her and as she felt a warm tear run down her face. She opened a box and hid them away.

One by one, the pirate picked up the treasures around the room. Some of them filled her with joy and beautiful memories and she kept them close. Some of them brought the feeling of pain or sorrow, and she continued to fill a box with those pieces. When she had completed sorting her treasures, she picked up the box that held all of those negative emotions and she carried it to the window and gently threw the box to the sea.

Immediately, the weight on her chest was lifted. She now felt peace in her cabin and she laid down on her soft bed and fell in to a restful sleep.

Captain's Log: The Captain's Quarters

It is important to know that each one of us, and everything else on this planet is vibrating. Some things just vibrate slowly enough that they feel solid. With those vibrations comes energy and energy always affects us, whether it is good or bad.

Look around your own living space. When you feel blocked or unhappy in your own space, the reason is usually because of the energy you are feeling. Take the time to go through your space, pick up each different object and note how those things make you feel. If you pick something up and it doesn't bring you joy, consider moving it to another space in your home or give it away.

While there are many objects that may pull your vibration down, there are other things that work to raise your vibration. It is always beneficial to bring the outside in. The Earth holds natural, clean energy and when we bring it into our homes, we will feel more grounded.

Crystals and rocks can be very beneficial. Crystals vibrate more slowly than we do, so keeping them around the home and holding on to them when we feel stressed, helps us to ground our energy and feel more centered and peaceful.

It is always important to be aware of how things affect your vibration. As you become more aware of how different objects affect you, you will learn how to create a space for yourself where you can thrive.

The Seagull

The captain watched the hungry little seagull as it squawked noisily in its cage. It was busy, so busy seeking more food that it never seemed to slow down long enough to notice the beauty around it.

He laughed at its antics. The bird reminded him of himself not so long ago. He too, was constantly busy seeking valuable treasures and never slowing down to listen to the waves as they hit the shore. The day came in this pirate's life when he woke up to the fact that he would never find enough treasure to make himself happy, for happiness would never lie in having more stuff. True happiness could only come from love. That was the day that he began to listen to that voice inside of him that sang a different song.

He slowed down, and he became quiet and in that solitude, he found himself.

Within each of us, lies two voices. There is the voice that seeks attention, that always wants to be heard, and there is a second voice that quietly waits to be discovered. This is the voice that comes to us in those moments of quiet reflection. It is in our own stillness, that we come to the realization that down inside we each have the voice of our true selves. This is the voice that has all of the answers we seek.

The captain was changed on the day that he began to seek the voice of his higher self. He remembered how his life had changed and he felt calm wash over him. He walked to the squawking bird and gave it a few treats and laughed as the bird, finally full, settled down to rest. Again, this bird taught him a lesson. That noisy voice that likes to steal the show is not so difficult to quiet. Like this seagull, it only seeks a full belly of love.

This is your lesson too. The secret to quieting your ego is a simple one. Feed it love, Pat it on the head and place it in a comfortable cage. Ego is an important part of who we are, but if it is not fed the love that it desires, it will squawk so loudly that it will drown out the voice of wisdom, peace and love. In order to step out of the chaotic world of your humanity, you must learn to give your ego a few treats and then gently put it back in its cage for a rest.

The Eye Patch

I do not wear a patch over one eye because I am missing that eye. I wear that patch because my life can jump from one extreme to the next very quickly. In any given moment, I may be bathing in the brightest light that the Universe has to offer, and in the next, darkness may flood over me.

My eye patch gives me the ability to adjust quickly to the changes. One eye covered, is always ready to see through extreme darkness while the other eye always **is** adjusted to the light.

A good pirate remembers his ability to look at things differently by simply moving his patch to the other eye. Suddenly, the eye that was used to viewing a world of darkness can experience a new light. It is all about where this pirate places the patch.

So it is with each one of us. In every moment, we make the choice to focus on what is ugly or what is beautiful. We can choose to see what is good in the world, or we can place our focus on all that is bad.

For lightworkers, we always have the choice to remain in the light or to walk through the darkness. No matter where you choose to place your focus, always remember that you have the ability to change how you view things by simply moving your patch to the other eye. You can always find your way back out of the darkness by simply letting in more light.

The Wheel

Each one of us holds command of our own pirate ship. We battle through storms, and we hold on too tightly to that wheel believing that if we let go, we will go someplace that we don't want to be. We couldn't be more wrong. For each one of us, there is a larger hand at work, ready to take the wheel and guide us to safer waters, if we will only learn to let go.

Your ship has stopped at a beautiful island. Picture yourself standing in front of a dam that is holding back a river of gold. There is a hole in the dam and you are standing before it with your finger in the hole as you keep the dam from breaking and releasing all of the treasure behind it. That gold represents everything you have coming to you, but you are holding it back, through guilt, doubt, and false belief. As soon as you can let go of negative emotion toward yourself, and pull your finger out of that hole, the dam will come crashing down and all of that treasure that is just waiting to be set free, will flow easily into your existence.

So many times, those of us who are highly sensitive, take on the belief that we are unworthy of a life that is filled with joy. We punish ourselves for past mistakes, or what we perceive as failures. We hold ourselves back, and when we do that we aren't only hurting ourselves, we are depriving the world of our own special gifts. We didn't come here to hide under a cloud of self-doubt, we came here to shine our lights so brightly that the darkness can no longer exist. You are worthy. You are so loved.

Every day, remind yourself that the only person that keeps you from abundance is you. Let go of the wheel and let your ship glide safely through still waters, right to the place, where all of your dreams will come true.

The Oar

As the pirates pulled the oars through the choppy sea, they felt the power of the current push and pull at their small vessel. They would naturally push against the strong current as it threatened to capsize them. Their bodies would lean from one side to the other as the oars touched the water. There was a perfect balance in the process and they performed with the ease that only came from many years at sea.

The captain watched as the tiny island came closer and closer into view. He felt a change on the horizon. Just as he was impressed by the crew's ability to balance the small boat, he also was impressed by their ability to find a balance in life. Gone were the days of chaos in search of plunder. Now there were those days of excitement and adventure, but in the midst of those days, were days like today, when they chose to find a peaceful place to throw down the anchor and go ashore for a rest from the wind and the waves.

The captain smiled at his crew. He knew that soon, there would be laughter and rum. The small island would come alive as they sang silly songs and danced around the campfire, and when the fun was done, there would come a rest under the gentle breezes and the full moon.

Life is all about balance. It is about the ultimate realization that you are a powerfully created spark of God, and then realizing that so is everyone else. It is about finding power in humility, strength in your compassion, and peace out of the chaos. It is about hard work, and then finding rest, and about finding joy out of sorrow.

We can't find a balance in our lives if **life** always **is** easy. There is power in contrasts. Through struggle we find peace. Through death we find life. Through sadness we find our bliss. For every pain there is promise. We only need to practice, in order to find the perfect balance. It is always there, waiting for us to bring it to the surface.

Above all, it is the simple revelation that we do not have to seek love because we are love. Love is never lost and it never dies. How can you lose what is essentially the very essence of who you are? You are a perfectly balanced vessel, able to withstand all of life's storms. Learning to accept your perfection is the first step in the realization that you are the master and commander of your life, and that nothing can pull you to the bottom of the sea without you giving it permission to do so.

The Candle

I n every Pirate's life there is great contrast. The brightest of days have a way of turning into the darkest of nights. It is important to always keep your candle ready.

It is a general misconception among lightworkers, that once we come in to the light, we will never again walk through any darkness. We will, and we do. Like the deepest of seas, our inner souls will always hide deep, dark mysteries to uncover.

As we come more fully into the light, we learn to place our focus on the brighter aspects of who we are more often than the dark ones. We should never forget that the darkness also has purpose.

Sometimes it is necessary to dive deeply into the depths of our own dark seas, in order to find those parts of ourselves that need to be brought up to the surface for healing. That process takes courage. It is never easy to search for the monsters that hide under the surface of our waters, but if we allow fear to stop us, the monsters continue to thrive and grow, until one day, they reach out of the depths of the sea and threaten to sink the entire ship.

Once you find your inner candle, it will never go out. It always is there to light your way on those dark journeys into the sea of your soul. Don't be afraid to dive down deep into your own darkness when you feel the need. No matter how deeply you are pulled into the dark waters, your candle will always be there to help you find your way back to the surface. None of us can fully claim the light until we are willing to dive in and fight our own demons. Hiding from our inner monsters will never make them go away. Go after each one and as you find them, put them each in their cages. The harder you work at this, the more you will realize that your monsters no longer control you.

Hold your candle strong. You are an amazing pirate. There is no monster that is powerful enough to destroy your light.

The Puzzle

The captain sat quietly in her quarters. Her life was never easy. The crew was always looking to her for all the answers and she needed a rest.

A candle burned nearby creating a soft light over the large puzzle that was laid out before her. It was beginning to take shape but there were still many loose pieces, and she wondered why she had chosen such a difficult task.

One by one, she picked up the pieces as she looked for the place where they would fit. She noticed that many of the pieces were bent from the times that she tried to force them in where they didn't belong.

She sat there in her quiet room, away from all of the noise up above, and listened to the comforting ticking of her clock. There was such peace in just being alone in this space. She thought about her life, and she realized that it was just like the puzzle that lay before her.

Living the life of a pirate was not an easy road. Many times, along the way, she had tried to fit the wrong pieces into the puzzle, and in the process, she was too was a bit frayed around the edges.

She realized that it was very difficult to see the beauty of the completed puzzle, while it still lay in pieces on the table. She had been working on this puzzle for a very long time, and what she now knew, was that on those days, when she took the time to become quiet, and allowed herself to be alone, the pieces just seemed to come together easily.

Her puzzle was not meant to be forced or rushed. She knew that eventually, all of the pieces would come together perfectly. If she was to create the masterpiece she desired, she would have to be still, in order to hear that voice inside of her that was always there to be her guide.

So it is with each one of us. We are each creating the most beautiful puzzles. When we look at the millions of pieces, we can become overwhelmed with the huge task. Many times, we try to force pieces into place, or we get angry and throw the pieces in the air.

What we have forgotten is that we are never required to create our masterpieces alone. Each one of us has that quiet knowing, that voice, that is always there to guide us through those days when we feel overwhelmed or lost at sea.

It is in becoming quiet, and looking within, that we suddenly see more clearly. Slow down, be still. Seek your answers from that quiet space inside of you. You will find that as you practice the skill of quiet reflection, your pieces fit more easily, and you will feel less frayed. A beautiful life will unfold for each one of us when we stop pushing so hard and simply allow it to fall into place.

The Lighthouse

The captain stood in front of the mirror looking at the heavy coat that she wore. This was the coat that showed the world what she had wanted them to see. It was a coat that covered her insecurities and scars. Safely hidden within the wool and buttons, she appeared strong and fierce. She couldn't even remember the day she had decided to wear this coat. It was like another lifetime and she had grown weary under the weight of it.

She slowly released the buttons and allowed the coat to fall to the floor. It was as if the weight of the world had been lifted from her, and she sighed in relief.

Her eyes were drawn to the wardrobe and she opened the doors to reveal the dress that she had worn before she had set it aside to take on the role of the pirate captain. She had forgotten that it was still there.

Tenderly, she reached out and ran her hands over the silky fabric. It felt as if the gown was made from the softest **sea** water as it flowed through her fingers.

Love flooded her soul as she remembered the girl that she was before she had grown so fierce and cold. She wondered if she could still wear this dress. She lifted her arms and allowed it to flow over her head, and in that simple action, she was transformed.

She looked at herself, and could see that the tough pirate was gone. The dress did not hide her scars the way the coat had, but those scars only brought more beauty. These were the marks of a woman who had survived all of life's storms and battles. They were not imperfections at all, they only made her more beautiful. The dress allowed her true self to shine and she realized that she had been wrong. It is not in hiding herself under those layers of protection that made her more worthy, of respect, it was in letting go of that heavy coat, that the world would see how truly amazing she really was.

She knew that it was time to allow a change. It was time to shine so brightly that she would be like a lighthouse in the darkness of a world that was lost at sea.

The coat would stay there on the floor. She would no longer be burdened under the weight of it. With the soft dress flowing gently around her, she stepped out of her cabin into a brand-new life.

Conclusion

N ow, that you have come to the end of this pirate adventure, I hope that you have begun to see the greatness that lies within you. This is the time for you to begin again.

Today, you are brand new. The old pains and losses have fallen away to reveal the beauty within.

Take a look at yourself and realize your own perfection. Think of everything that you have lived through, every mistake that you think you have made, and realize that it was all just experience.

Those things were only there to help you grow. They do not control you. Now that you have finally unveiled the amazing creation that you are, you can pack up all of those painful memories and cast them aside.

Close your eyes and imagine a storm front on your horizon. There is no fear in the change it brings. There is a cool breeze pulling those clouds over your life. They bring rain to wash you clean. They bring water to fill your buckets. They bring wind to fill your sails. They bring a new life that is filled with hope, with dreams, and above all, they bring adventure out on the open seas.

Spread your sails to the sky and allow your life to unfold before you. Let today be the first day of the rest of your life.

CPSIA information can be obtained
at www.ICGtesting.com
Printed in the USA
LVOW06s1515281117
557719LV00009B/151/P